INSIDE A RECOVERING HEART

By Kelly Baughman

(a personal look at spiritual formation and recovery with reflective questions to guide you along the way)

Copyright © 2015 by Kelly Baughman

Inside a Recovering Heart
(a personal look at spiritual formation and recovery with reflective questions to guide you along the way)
by Kelly Baughman

Printed in the United States of America.

ISBN 9781498440127

All rights reserved solely by the author. The author guarantees all contents are original and do not infringe upon the legal rights of any other person or work. No part of this book may be reproduced in any form without the permission of the author. The views expressed in this book are not necessarily those of the publisher.

Scripture quotations taken from the New International Version (NIV). Copyright © 1973, 1978, 1984, 2011 by Biblica, Inc.™. Used by permission. All rights reserved.

www.xulonpress.com

TABLE OF CONTENTS

FOREWORD	vii
DEDICATION	ix
ACKNOWLEDGMENT	xi
PREFACE	xv
IN THE BEGINNING	19
Childhood	19
Adulthood	24
Reflection/Discussion Questions	29
A TURNING POINT	31
Going to Camp	31
Reflection/Discussion Questions	38
YOUNG ADULTHOOD	39
I'm Falling	39
The Quiet Stranger	44
Reflection/Discussion Questions	48
EARLY MARRIAGE AND FAMILY	49
Joys and Challenges	49
Reflection/Discussion Questions	55
OUT OF CONTROL	57
Sickness	57

Submission 62
    Reflection/Discussion Questions 64
GRIEVING, SPIRITUAL FORMATION,
AND RECOVERY 67
    Life after Death 67
    Reentry troubles 72
    Reflection/Discussions Questions 78
MOVING FORWARD 79
    Making Changes 79
    Reflection/Discussion Questions 88
BUMPS IN THE ROAD 91
    Clouds from the Past 91
    Reflection/Discussion Questions 96
HUNGER AND THIRST 97
    Journey with Gratitude. 97
WHAT DOES THIS MEAN? 101
    Questions from "Inside of
    Recovering Hearts" 101
HOW IMPORTANT IS THIS STUFF?
    The Peacock Feather 117

FINAL THOUGHTS 119
INSIDE <u>YOUR</u> RECOVERING HEART (additional
questions to guide you along your path) 121
APPENDIX A–Another Step 125
APPENDIX B–Influences and Resources 127

FOREWORD

Kelly speaks honestly and passionately to all of us who have dealt with hurts and habits in our life from childhood into adulthood. He guides us to look at our own lives, face the wounds, and seek the Lord for freedom and hope.

I have walked alongside him down many roads. I have entered into tough conversations with him, cried, yelled, pushed him away, and pulled him close. May you find peace as you connect your story to this story and allow the Lord to take you into His care because He loves you. Praise God for His incredible works!

Kathy Baughman

DEDICATION:

This book is dedicated to my wife Kathy, who has walked with me through much of my journey and has consistently shown me God's love and grace along the way.

ACKNOWLEDGEMENTS:

I am particularly grateful to my family and friends who hold a special place in my heart and who have impacted my life immensely, more than they probably realize. Also, I am grateful to the hundreds of individuals who have walked with me through the hills and valleys of life. I believe God has used each of you in my life for a special purpose. Thank you.

I am so very grateful for the many men and women I have walked with in their recovery process. You have helped me look deeper into my own life.

I am most grateful to God. It is through my Lord and Savior Jesus Christ and the work of God's Spirit that this book exists. He has never given up on me.

SPECIAL RECOGNITION:

Kathy Baughman, Brad Baughman, Heidi Baughman, Jacob Baughman, Matt Knighton Senior, Roland Classen, and Tim Young for reading my manuscript and providing much needed insight and encouragement.

Melissa Baughman (1987-1994) for making a significant impact in my life and the lives of many others, even though she didn't live very long on this earth.

Editor:
Allisyn Ma

PREFACE

The patients waited for me to begin my talk. Their staring eyes reflected lives of brokenness, deception, guilt, and shame. I had agreed to provide a "spirituality" lecture for the patients at a local drug and alcohol recovery center located at the hospital where I was serving as a healthcare chaplain. Although I wrestled with the content and approach, I found myself sitting in a large circle of men and women struggling with various forms of addiction. I found myself intimidated by their raw emotions and for many, an intense desire to make permanent changes in their lives. My insecurity set in. I didn't feel adequate or competent enough to help these people. I quietly prayed to God. I asked Him to intervene in what I was to share with these people.

Then it occurred to me that the eyes staring at me were, in many ways, a reflection of myself. Each man and woman in that circle represented a journey, a spiritual journey. The reflections in their eyes gave me a glimpse into their hearts. They were desperately seeking for hope when their lives seemed hopeless. The feelings of intimidation and insecurity subsided, and I began to share with them, not as an "expert" in the field of recovery (which I am not), but as a fellow sojourner on the road from brokenness to freedom, from hurt to hope.

It has been several years since I gave that first lecture at the recovery center, and I have shared that same lecture every month since then. Literally hundreds of patients have heard it and many have responded with gratitude and an intense desire to continue seeking God and allowing Him to invade their hearts with the gift of hope. This book has been inspired by that response. It reflects the principles of that lecture, albeit more extensively.

It is with gratitude and joy that I share this book with all of you. In many ways we are all in recovery. We are recovering from the effects of specific habits, compulsions, and/or coping behaviors that have held us captive for much of our lives. We are recovering, or desiring to recover, from our bondage and the consequences of sin (rebellion and disobedience from God), and many of us are recovering from a painful loss or series of losses we've experienced in our life. We are broken people with a deep desire to live a life of freedom, hope, and wholeness.

A good portion of this book is my story. It's an inside look at my heart as I have journeyed through life. It's a

Preface

story of spiritual formation and recovery. I'll give you a glimpse into the heart of many addicts, alcoholics, and grieving patients as I address many of their questions around the theme of spirituality and recovery. I suggest that in order to get the most out of this book, you pause periodically and spend time reflecting on your own life. I have included some reflection questions at the end of each section. These questions could be used as prompts for journal entries or in small discussion groups.

I've included additional questions at the end of the book that might help you take a closer look at your spiritual formation and recovery process. Whether you use the questions or not, it will be important that you read this with the intent of reflecting on your own life and taking a closer "inside-look" into your heart and allowing God's Spirit to move you closer to that place of freedom, hope, and wholeness.

May God give you a purpose in reading this, and may He use this book to help you move forward through the hills and valleys, the joys and sorrows, and down the often rugged path we call life. Reflect with me. Cry with me. Pray with me. Hope with me. Join me on the inside… "Inside a Recovering Heart."

Kelly Baughman

IN THE BEGINNING

CHILDHOOD

*I*n the beginning, there were wheat fields. The small eastern Washington farm town where I grew up had a population of 400-500 people along with the many dogs, cats, horses, and the occasional goat. My earliest recollections of life events that made an impact on my spiritual formation are in and around this small town. Although, I later grew to understand that my spirituality began prior to being born, spiritual formation is a journey that often cannot be seen without reflecting back on your life. It is all of the moments that God pushed me in the direction of becoming who I am today, of how He has grown me.

I was not raised in a religious home. In fact, I don't recall even saying prayers before meals or praying as a family at all, for that matter. Faith was seen as a private issue within my family. However, I do recall going periodically to a little Presbyterian church and attending Sunday school from time to time and walking to church with my cousins a few days during the summer to attend a Vacation Bible School, a week-long summer program for kids.

I attended church on Christmas Eve and most Easter Sundays. My family and I dressed up in our finest clothes. For me, that meant a white shirt and a bow tie. We went to a small church, which seemed to seat about a quarter of the town on these special days. We sat in the well-used pews, heard the biblical account of either Christmas or Easter (depending on the season), sang some themed hymns, and went home or to my aunt and uncle's house for some holiday treats. My sister and brother and I often spent time playing with things in the pews during the sermon. I enjoyed listening to the choir and the solo vocalists, especially my uncle who I thought was an incredible singer.

My family and I still laugh as we think back to a Christmas Eve service when my dad, who was taking a German class in college at the time, joined the congregation in singing "Silent Night" at the conclusion of the service. He not only sang a few off-key notes, but he also had attempted to sing in German. His singing echoed through the sanctuary (at least that is how I remember it). My siblings and I were devastated, to say the least, and dad was probably bruised from the numerous elbow jabs he received from my mom.

My understanding of spiritual ideas was influenced by the Bible stories I heard in Sunday school throughout my childhood. Granted, many of the stories seemed to be totally unrelated to each other but they often spoke about God, or the work of God, which influenced my curiosity and even provided some understanding of who I was as a spiritual being.

The pastor's wife, who was my Sunday school teacher, had a lasting impact on my life when I was about 5 or 6 years old. She was a very caring, nurturing lady. I remember the love I felt from her, especially when she allowed me to place figurines on a flannel storyboard as she told a Bible story. I also remember her allowing me to march around the room with the class and sing my favorite song, "Onward Christian Soldiers." Thinking back, I can see how loving, caring relationships are a vital part in one's spiritual growth.

Although my religious activities were limited in my early years, I have fond memories of my childhood experiences in that little country church.

At a very early age, I recall gazing outside during clear summer nights with wonder and curiosity. I developed a deep sense that there existed some kind of supernatural power that created and sustained the stars, planets, nature, and many things that have never made sense to me. I remember being introduced to the idea, through random Bible stories, that there existed a power that seemed to make significant changes in people's lives, and a power that had something to do with love. I experienced this through my interactions with people, and it was reinforced as I learned songs like "Jesus Loves Me."

The process of questioning and wondering about many of life's mysteries, such as death and the afterlife, allowed me to wrestle with spiritual issues and concepts. I remember walking with my friend around our small town carrying our BB guns. We would shoot at the barn swallows or the frogs in the nearby creek, like a Huck Finn story. One day my friend shot and killed a dove. It fell to the ground, and instead of celebrating, we both felt sad. We decided to bury the dove in my yard. I don't know why we felt compassion for the dove, but I remember looking at it, a beautiful bird and relating it to God and the Bible in some way (probably from the Noah's Ark story). Following the dove's burial, we talked about the dove's afterlife. I don't recall what we talked about specifically, but I remember that the discussion was way more serious than any we'd had before. The process of questioning and wondering about God's creation and afterlife was a meaningful part of my early spiritual journey.

My family influenced my spiritual formation, as well. My parents dedicated themselves to raising me, and even though I was impacted by their personal hurts and habits, as we all are, I was shaped by their love as well. As I mentioned before, I wasn't raised in a religious home, but my parents did demonstrate parental love and care to me, which provided me with a framework as I gradually began to wrestle with the theological concept of a loving God. They modeled and reinforced values that proved, over time, to create in me strong moral character traits. They taught me the value of family, hard work, responsibility, respect, interest in people, and relationships, just to name a few.

First relationships are an important part of one's spiritual formation. I was the oldest of three kids, followed by my sister, then my brother. We were two years apart in age, so we grew to know each other pretty well. We faced each other's good, bad, and ugly sides throughout our years under the same roof. Together we waded through the highs and lows of living life together. We helped each other, hurt each other, laughed together, and cried together. At times, we caused each other pain, yet we also learned to forgive and reconcile our differences.

My family was clearly the meaningful core of those in direct contact with me as I wrestled my way through the early years of life. It is through them that I first experienced love, forgiveness, and commitment.

I would have to say that even the community of people where I was raised formed me spiritually. Upon reflection, it is evident that many of the community members in my small town helped me move toward God through their acts of love and lives of moral integrity as they pursued God. Yet others pulled me away from God through their modeling of "justified" rebellion and negative behaviors, but either way they definitely influenced my life.

My spiritual formation began early in life. I can look back now and see how God was seeking after me from the earliest years. Although I was not aware of it at the time, He pursued me, He loved me, and He was always there.

It seemed like overnight my body grew, rapidly and disproportionately. My thinking skills were overrun by my emotions, and my interests began to change. This next phase of life would bring significant challenges and crossroads to face.

Adolescence

I can pretty much sum up my adolescent years in five words: sports, music, girls, parties, work. I am not sure how I would place these in an order of importance in my life, though I am most certain work would be at the bottom of my list. Notice that I didn't place God or any spiritual matters as a priority in my life at all. God wasn't mentioned because the other things (sports, girls, parties, music) were my "gods." It is not that God wasn't at work in my life, because I am most certain He was, but I didn't pay attention to Him.

I recklessly navigated through my adolescent years during the 1970s. If you know a bit about history, you know that those were some interesting years, to say the least. Well, I was a part of the '70s, which most definitely included sexual promiscuity, parties with a lot of alcohol, and sports idolatry. I did go to church occasionally, but to be honest, my primary motive in going was to see my guy friends and the girls.

I do remember when a youth group was formed at our church. A hip young couple from an outlying college gathered a few teens together on a week night and sang some folk-style songs with us as they played on the guitar. Then they attempted to lead us in meaningful discussions about life, God, and relationships. I enjoyed it. At the time, it seemed so different than anything I was used to. But honestly, the big attraction of youth group was flirting with girls, messing around with friends, and the dinner we had each week. However, I didn't attend the group very much because my god was actually sports, and it consumed the bulk of my time and energy.

However, I did attend a youth group retreat where I learned more of what I was learning at youth group, but in an outdoor setting. I got more practice at flirting with girls, messing around with friends, and eating.

By all outward appearances my life was void of God during my early adolescent years, and in many ways it is true. I really had very little interest in spirituality. Although I developed a definite belief that God was big, powerful, and that He loved me, I couldn't explain what that meant.

I can see how at an early age God placed a sincere compassion in my heart for people in need. I had a deep rooted desire to help people, something that God nurtured and used in later years of my life. In fact, I remember feeling drawn to people who were mentally or physically disadvantaged. There were times when kids at school teased and harassed some of the kids that struggled with learning disabilities, and I recall feeling a sincere empathy for the victims. At times, I made an attempt to convince the kids to stop their bullying, but many times I just let it happen, then later provided comfort to the victim. I really struggled with situations like these because not only did I have a true compassion for hurting people, but I also struggled very deeply with pleasing others and avoiding conflicts. So, when situations like these came around, I <u>often tried passively</u> (usually through the use of humor) to make everything work out for everyone.

Although my church involvement was limited during adolescence, I found it comforting to attend church. There were many people in church who seemed to care about me for no particular reason. I didn't feel like I had to perform, particularly in sports, in order for them to have an interest in me. Even though I mainly went to church to socialize, I liked the feeling I got from church. I even liked getting dressed up on Sunday mornings, especially on Easter. It was showing my respect for God. Unfortunately, there were many Sunday mornings I didn't go to church because I was out late at a party on Saturday night, and I was often very tired or hungover.

From preadolescence on, music became important to me. Growing up, music was always playing in our house. As a child and throughout my adolescent years, pop rock was the music of choice for my parents and me. I loved the rhythm of music. It seemed to do something inside me. It made me feel alive and connected. It is no wonder that I began playing drums at a very early age. It helped to have some basic lessons from my dad, a former drummer. I did not understand it at the time, but I came to realize, years later, the impact music and rhythm can have on one's spiritual formation. God created sounds and rhythms. They are part of His design.

In fact, there seems to be a rhythm and rhyme to the way He designed the universe, the seasons, stages of life, the heartbeat, and so forth. It is no wonder that for thousands of years, rhythm and music are one of the ways the human race has expressed praise and worship back to God.

As I mentioned, sports and music were like gods to me, and I listened to music and played sports all the time. If I wasn't playing sports or listening to music (even while playing the drums), I was searching for drinking parties or girls, or working in the wheat fields. It was actually through working the wheat fields and grain elevators that I earned enough money to participate in a couple of different weeklong summer basketball camps. The first camp I attended was between my sophomore and junior year of high school. It was put on at a local university and helped me improve my overall game.

The other camp was the one that changed my life though, and it took place by a local lake. It was put on by a former college coach, who had recently started the camp. He came to our school and promoted the camp to all of the athletes. He challenged a few of us guys by saying that we would most likely have a difficult time with the intensity of the camp. He didn't think we could handle it. The coach made it clear that if someone got through his camp, they would not only be winners on the court, but they would be winners in life as well. He got our attention. So between my junior and senior year, I attended this weeklong camp. This proved to be a major turning point in my spiritual life.

Reflection/Discussion Questions:

1. Psalm 139:13-14 states, "For you [God] created my inmost being; you knit me together in my mother's womb. I praise you because I am fearfully and wonderfully made; your works are wonderful, I know full well." What does this suggest about your early spiritual formation?
2. What childhood life events or people influenced your spiritual direction?
3. How were your family and/or community influential in forming your spiritual direction?
4. How would you summarize your adolescent years? What were your priorities in life? How did you pursue these priorities?
5. Although the author had very little to do with God during his early adolescent years, he claimed to have a core belief that God was big and powerful and loved him. Do you recall what you believed about God during your adolescent years? What informed your belief up to that point in your life?

TURNING POINT

GOING TO CAMP

I arrived at the basketball camp feeling pretty exhausted. I had spent the night before the camp at a late night party. Oh yes, I was exhausted and a bit hungover, but I figured that I would run off the alcohol, which I most definitely did. I discovered that this camp was going to be a real challenge. The coaches at the camp worked me harder than I had ever worked in my life, and I actually discovered that I liked it. It felt good to be pushed. It felt good to be absolutely exhausted from mental and physical exercise by the end of the day. It felt good to be challenged emotionally and spiritually.

Every evening, following a long hard day on the outdoor courts, which were blazing hot from the eastern Washington sun, we sat down for a nightly program. Following announcements, there were humorous skits and inspirational sports videos. Periodically, the leader would teach us some motivational chants. The program closed with a special speaker whose message highlighted the theme of the evening. It seemed like the theme of the night varied (family, friendships, positive attitude, et cetera).

However, I will never forget my last night there. The speaker was one of the coaches. He had an intense passion and an authentic personality. He had a warm loving, "tough love" kind of heart. He got my attention right off the bat, and he didn't lose my attention the entire time he spoke. His topic was the theme of a relationship with God. He made the point that our spiritual life is integrated into everything we do and not just at Sunday school or church. He was explaining, with great enthusiasm and sincerity that God not only loved us, but He also knows us personally. His talk began to penetrate my heart. It was like he spoke directly to me. He made a point to tell us that the Creator God not only knows everything that I do and think, but He still loves me, which produced an intense combination of guilt and hope in my mind and heart.

The speaker held my attention that night. You see, when I entered the camp it appeared to me that the staff acted differently. They seemed to possess an exaggerated sense of enthusiasm and joy. They appeared confident and passionate about life. They had the courage to not only share their faith in God but to demonstrate their conviction through their acts of love and kindness. These coaches got my attention from day one of camp. Admittedly, at first I thought they were phonies, you know, hypocrites. I thought they were trying to be something they were not. But as the week went on, the more I realized these guys were very authentic. They were the real deal; and the bottom line was, whatever they had I wanted! Deep down in my heart, I wanted joy, peace, confidence, courage, and conviction. I wanted to know for certain that I was loved by God, especially after all of the sinful decisions I had made day in and day out. I wanted what the coaches appeared to have, and the speaker was now telling me how to do this.

The speaker went on that night to tell the gymnasium full of athletes how to turn their lives around. He explained how each of us has a void in our heart that is yearning to be filled. He shared examples of what an empty heart looks like and feels like, and boy I could relate. He explained how his whole life had changed. Then, with passionate conviction that I had never witnessed, he made the claim that in order to change, one must ask God for forgiveness and then intentionally invite Him into their life. He made a point that if one really wants to make a change – a permanent change – it must begin with a real personal relationship with God, available through His Son, Jesus Christ.

The speaker gave all of us athletes an opportunity to commit our lives to Jesus, to ask Him to become our Lord and Savior, and to have an authentic, day to day relationship with Him. I remember thinking to myself: "Wow, this is all there is to it. All I have to do is ask Jesus into my life and I will be changed." I remember another side of me saying: "Well, if I commit my life to Jesus, then I will not be able to live the life that I am living now." The thought made me feel lonely. I liked my friends at home, and I didn't want to give them up. They understood me. But on the other hand, I wanted to change my ways. I really wanted to become a different person. I really believed that deep down I was living an empty life, and the void in my life was the absence of a sincere relationship with God.

So, the internal conflict continued that Thursday evening as the speaker talked about the possibilities of having a changed life. Finally, when he was nearly finished speaking, the coach provided an opportunity for any of us to come to the front of the gymnasium, in front of our peers, and pray to God for forgiveness and invite Jesus into our lives.

Sweat poured off of me when he gave the invitation, and I am not sure what, or who, got a hold of me (I later learned it was the work of the Holy Spirit in my life), but I walked forward and stood in front of my peers, prayed, and invited Jesus into my life. A half-dozen other guys joined me. We then allowed the speaker to pray for us, and the rest of the athletes applauded as we sat back down in our seats. I thought to myself that my life had now changed. That was it. I was now a new creation, according to the speaker. I immediately felt a sense of peace and confidence.

We went back to our cabins that evening and gathered with our roommates and the cabin leader to discuss the day and to follow up from the speaker's message. The topic that night was the theme of making a decision to invite Jesus into our life. I became the central point in the evening discussion since I was the only one from our cabin that had made that commitment. It seemed like everyone else already had committed their lives to God. I felt like I had entered into a foreign world. Most of the others in the cabin carried Bibles, and they actually knew where to find verses and specific Bible stories. Some of my cabin friends were overly enthusiastic in their attempts to guide me in my new journey with God. I listened respectfully to them and hoped I would do what they were suggesting, but deep down I knew that soon I would be going back to my world. I would be surrounded by parties, girls, work, and sports. I felt that the world of

Bible reading, regular church attendance, and abstaining from sinful behaviors, especially in the area of lust and sexual promiscuity, would be very difficult, if not impossible, to accomplish.

Prior to going to sleep that night, I thought about my friends back home. I tried to reason out how I could keep my friends and at the same time live in a new way. I prayed to God. The prayer seemed different this time. It felt like God was really with me, in fact, deep within me. It felt good. Something had changed me that week at camp. I reflected back on my arrival at camp (hungover from an all-night drinking binge) and then leaving with Jesus in my life and a small "Mr. Hustle" trophy, awarded to me at the end of camp.

I went back home to my friends and family. I finished up the wheat harvest for the end of the summer and began training for football season.

I was ready to take on the world. I was a changed young man! I had Jesus in my life. I no longer needed to use tobacco or misuse alcohol or women. I was ready to walk with integrity. I had a sincere desire to behave like the coaches at camp with enthusiasm, confidence, courage, and love. I didn't feel ready to carry around my Bible everywhere I went, like the guys at camp, but I was ready to have my Bible on my bedroom desk, available to read. In fact, I found myself reading the Bible in the evenings before falling asleep. I began to pray before sleeping as well. In the past, I only used to pray before sports events, in church, or when I was in trouble, and I never read the Bible.

I was really a new man, not just on the inside, but on the outside as well. I behaved like I thought a follower of Jesus should behave. I shared my new experience, my changed life, with my family and friends. My family was happy that I'd had a good camp experience. They supported my newfound attitude and behavior. I shared my new life journey with a girl I was seeing. She also was glad I'd had a good camp experience. I shared with some of my friends. They were interested in the sports part of camp, but it seemed like they really didn't get the "God thing." They didn't grasp the heartfelt change I had experienced at camp. They didn't get that this "relationship with God" thing was very real, and I had it.

I felt positive and confident. I was looking forward to starting school in the fall. I was prepared to enter the school year as a new man. I looked forward to beginning the football season with a different perspective. I was excited to approach sports, not as a god or an idol to be worshiped, but instead as a way or means to demonstrate the talent that God gave me. I was ready to play sports for God, not for me, and not for others.

Reflection/Discussion Questions:

1. During your adolescent years, did you ever have a memorable experience (positive or negative) that significantly impacted your spiritual life? Explain.
2. Have you ever had something in your life that you valued as a god or an idol?
3. The Bible tells us, "God so loved the world that He gave His one and only Son, that whoever believes in Him will not perish but have eternal life" (John 3:16). How would believing and acting on this statement impact one's spiritual condition?
4. Why do you think it is difficult for people to make a public commitment to God? Have you ever had a similar experience? What did you do? What did you feel?

YOUNG ADULTHOOD

I'M FALLING...

I began my senior year strong and confident. I made a commitment to walk the path of faith and in so doing, I developed a desire to change my behavior. The first thing that changed was my use of profanity. After I committed my life to God at camp, I stopped using profanity. My bad habit of swearing in conversations, especially with friends, plain and simply stopped. It didn't happen progressively or as a matter of "willing it away," it just didn't seem right or natural for me to swear anymore. This permanent change gave clear evidence to me that God was doing something in my life.

I desired to stop using tobacco and alcohol. I attempted (with very limited success) to stop using chewing tobacco (something I began in 5th grade), and although I didn't stop drinking alcohol, I limited my intake to a few beers.

I called it "social drinking." Another behavior change I felt compelled to work on was not being sexually motivated and manipulative as I interacted with girls.

My new attitude and behavior was a great way to start my senior year, and my friends accepted it. Yet, it seemed like they weren't taking me seriously. Many treated me like I was simply going through some kind of phase, or I was becoming one of those religious nuts (a phrase that we used in reference to the "Jesus people" – a societal movement beginning to grow at our school).

Contrary to my initial expectation, it didn't take long for me to slide back into my old ways. I had been sucked back into the dark side. No one made me go there; I was attracted to the dark side. I didn't realize, or even think about how difficult a committed faith would be. I sincerely believed that God was with me and had miraculously begun to transform me and would finish what He had started. That's what I wanted. I had no idea that I had a part in this process. I honestly thought that if I received Jesus into my life, then somehow, almost like magic, Jesus would ZAP me, and I would be like the coaches at camp. I would not continually lust or drink excessively every weekend, but rather would pursue a life of integrity, confidence, courage, and peace. Needless to say I entered into a time of spiritual crisis. I began to choose off-roading instead of the main path. In fact, the trails I

Young Adulthood

chose led me into a spiritual tailspin, or better yet, a spiritual train wreck.

I began to live a double life, a Jekyll and Hyde lifestyle, which I found to be horribly emotionally and spiritually deadening. I intentionally behaved in two completely different ways.

One could argue that all of us do this to some degree, and that is probably accurate, but in my case, at this time in my life, other than not using profanity, I intentionally behaved in ways that I knew were contrary to God's design and purpose. Yet, privately, usually in my bedroom, I would make an effort to stay on good terms with God. I prayed often for forgiveness and made an effort to read sections of the Bible. I didn't enjoy reading at the time, so reading the Bible was a real challenge, to say the least. I often read verses from the book of Psalms or Proverbs because I overheard someone at camp explain how helpful it was to them. I really didn't understand what I was reading, but I found a few verses to be very encouraging and challenging. The book of Proverbs is a book of wisdom, and is all about our attitudes, thought life, and behaviors. It became clearer to me that much of my life was not pleasing to God. The double life I was living became very evident, and it came to a point where I had to make a decision regarding my daily choices.

I told myself that either I should live my life for God or not. I had to directly face this dilemma when I was offered potential basketball scholarships to a couple of small Christian colleges. I was glad to receive interest from colleges because I really didn't know what I was going to do with my life. Academics were not a priority for me, so my high school grades were poor. In fact, if it wasn't for basketball, I'm not sure I would have gone to college at all.

The one college that was highly interested in me, made it clear that there was no alcohol or tobacco allowed on campus and there were no co-ed dorms. This was a big deal to me because it forced me to ask the questions: Am I ready to commit my whole life to God? Am I ready to live a clean life?

Initially the answer was yes, but it was so difficult for me to envision myself actually making those kinds of radical changes.

I turned away the idea of attending a Christian college and began to pursue other colleges. I obtained a basketball scholarship at a secular community college where I began my college career. The college allowed me to attend their school with my low high school grade point average because I was playing basketball, and I was willing to enroll in an entry level remedial English class and a study skills class.

This became another big turning point in my life.

I concluded that I wanted God in my life, but I didn't want to live according to His standards. I found myself choosing the double life. It slowly became my approach to life and let me tell you, it was very dark and miserable. On the surface, my public mask appeared to be confident and secure but privately I was a mess. I spent many nights in tears, crying out to God to help me change my ways.

I spent one year playing basketball at the small community college, then gave up basketball and went to a four year university, which, by the way, was a huge loss in my life. You must understand that during this time in my life, basketball was a god to me. My hopes and dreams for the future depended upon my athletic success. Actually, when I think about it, my identity, self-worth, and purpose were based on my basketball achievement. Coming to the realization that I was not as good as I thought I was, devastated me. Giving up my god left a hole in me. It was a deep internal wound, and I grieved in the way that I knew best... consuming alcohol and partying. The partying only masked my problem as I became more and more lost.

While at the university, my spiritual life took a distant backseat in terms of life priorities. I spent nearly three years studying, which miraculously I grew to enjoy, partying, and womanizing. Yet, I often spent private time in turmoil and desperately praying for forgiveness. There were times that the guilt of my actions from the night before drew me toward a state of depression. But I would get up the next day and do it all over again. The more I pursued this lifestyle, the less time I spent getting to know God.

Every weekend, and sometimes even in the middle of the week, I partied. After a while it got to a point where I didn't feel any guilt as a result of my inappropriate and promiscuous behavior, though previously, I would have felt some remorse and guilt. I was living a life without a moral conscience. I just didn't care anymore. I had spiraled out of control. I was willing to take more unhealthy risks with my life, especially while under the influence of alcohol.

I worked as a general labor worker at a local fruit and vegetable factory during the graveyard shift. It was one of a few part-time jobs I held throughout my college years. The job wasn't bad, but the hours interfered with my social life. When I did get an evening off, I tried to make up for lost time, and I spent all night partying until something happened.

THE QUIET STRANGER

Following an all-night binge, I went to work at the factory. During my lunch break, I began talking to a college-aged man. He was quietly sitting in the corner, eating lunch and reading a book. I don't know what got into me (I realize now that it was the work of the Holy Spirit), but I sat next to the man and began a conversation, which started out superficially, but soon changed into a life changing conversation. I began to share with him my own spiritual journey up until that point in my life. Maybe I was seeking encouragement, or perhaps was simply fishing for some common ground. Whatever the motivation, I ended up sharing.

The conversation was one dimensional. It was all about me. After a while, I asked him what he was reading. He was reading the Bible and briefly shared how relevant it was to his life. Deep down I wanted what he had. The feeling was similar to what I'd experienced at basketball camp.

I spent a good portion of our talk admitting my spiritual turmoil. I shared the pain of living a double life, and I shared a desire to get my life right with God. I was expecting the man to give me some kind of guilt lecture or mini sermon, but instead he said something that made an enormous impact on my life. He said, "God has not left you, you have left Him. He has been waiting for you to come back to Him." Our conversation concluded as he gave me a couple of Bible verses to read on my own: Matthew 15: 11-31, the story of the Prodigal Son, and

Hebrews 13:5, "I will never leave you nor forsake you." Lunch break was over, and we went our separate ways, forever. He got another job, and I never saw him again. It's amazing how God works through "random" people.

    I allowed the man's comment to penetrate deep into my heart and mind throughout the rest of the summer. Then one evening, I found a quiet place in the house, knelt on my knees, and began to have a heart-to-heart talk with God. I felt weak and vulnerable as I confessed my sinful behaviors. My eyes flooded with tears as I admitted how wrong I was in walking away from Him and how unworthy I felt that He would even consider still receiving me. The conversation was candid and honest. I don't know how long I was there, but I cried so much that I don't think I had another tear left. Finally, as I sat in silence, I sensed God's peace and comfort. I stood up and walked slowly out into the world. Once again, I felt like a changed man, a man who had been spiritually cleansed.

    The following three or four weeks I spent a great deal of time in the quietness of nature, usually at a local lake or beside a creek. In these moments of solitude, I talked to God about specific aspects of my broken life. God spoke to my heart in a new way. He made it clear that I had to break some negative patterns, beginning with how I used my leisure time. I told my party friends about the change in my life, but they were skeptical. However, the more they witnessed how serious I was, the more they accepted the change.

I cared for my friends, but over time I found myself spending less and less time with them. I went to fewer parties, never overdrank, and thought about and treated women a lot differently. Instead of seeing them as another pleasure object, I saw them as God's creation, worthy of love and respect. In fact, I began seeing all of God's creation in a similar way. I gained a new appreciation for the beauty of nature as I spent time jogging, walking, or simply praying at parks or by lakes. The core of my life was really beginning to change, which had a significant impact on my life, purpose, and direction.

I continued spending time alone with God. The Bible began to make more sense to me, and I began attending a local church. As I nurtured my soul, my confidence and self-assurance grew as well.

It was during this time that the university needed me to declare a major, and I knew that I wanted to dedicate my life to helping others. I looked into becoming a social worker or a probation officer, but after observing a local elementary school for a week, I fell in love with the children. God spoke to me through the energy, enthusiasm, and lives of the kids. I wanted to help others by having an influence in the lives of young people. I chose to major in education. I became a teacher and gradually received a master's degree in education. I've enjoyed teaching for many years. It is amazing how God directs our paths. I am so thankful that He doesn't give up on us.

Reflection/Discussion Questions:

1. Have you ever chosen "off-road trails" as you have journeyed through life? Tell your story. Describe what you mean by "off-road trails"? How would you describe your spiritual condition at the time?
2. How would you describe a double life? Have you ever intentionally lived this way?
3. The Bible tells us that God will never leave us (Hebrew 13:5). Can you give examples from your life? How you do you know this to be true? Share with someone.
4. Oftentimes we don't recognize losses that are not deaths as significant events in our lives. What are some of the losses you have faced, other than the death of a loved one? How did you grieve these losses?
5. Have you ever had a "quiet stranger" speak into your life (through words or deeds) and influence your spiritual direction? What made your interaction with this person influential? Share your story.

EARLY MARRIAGE AND FAMILY

JOYS AND CHALLENGES

I had my eye on a girl named Kathy for at least a year. She had seen me at some of the parties around campus and found my behaviors unattractive, to say the least. But she began to notice that now things were different. She recognized some changes in my actions. Although we didn't discuss the changes, she believed something was different about me. We started dating, and I enjoyed getting to know her. We shared some common values about family and spirituality. We shared a similar faith background: we both grew up in the same denominational tradition. As well, her family was loving and accepting of me and provided me with a fresh look at what a Christian family could look like.

Inside a Recovering Heart

Kathy and I enjoyed doing simple things together like going for walks, canoeing, going to basketball games, and attending social events. Back then, Kathy was not attending church, but she was willing to go with me on Sundays. She seemed to be very confident and self-assured, which were not strengths of mine, but one of the most important things I noticed was her heartfelt sense of grace. She didn't judge the way I used to behave. She loved and respected me, and I loved and respected her.

We saw each other quite frequently for three months. We got engaged and were to be married a year later as I began my first teaching job.

We started our life in a small logging community where I began teaching at a middle school and coaching sports teams. Life was new. Life was simple. Life was unknown. We dreamed together and began our family. Brad was our first. By the way, as the children grew, I discovered that humility and self-sacrifice were character qualities that definitely needed further development in my life, and being a father provided plenty of opportunities to grow in these areas.

One day while I was coaching basketball in an adjacent town, I received the urgent news that Brad, two months old at the time, needed to undergo surgery. Kathy and I thought he had the flu, but he was actually suffering from pyloric stenosis, a blockage from the stomach to the intestines, and needed immediate surgery. This was our first family crisis.

We had another child, Melissa, about two years later and excitedly brought her to our new home.

We began attending a small Presbyterian church in town. I had a growing desire to serve God, so I became the churches part-time youth leader. I knew the kids since I taught school in the community, but I was not theologically equipped or properly prepared to be a spiritual leader. However, I did the best I could. It felt right to be serving God, though I was certain that being a church youth leader would not be the way I would serve Him for long.

Since I was the high school girls' basketball coach as well as a teacher and coach at the middle school and now the youth leader, I had an influence on many of the kids in the community. I had an intense desire to make a long-term spiritual impact on the kids' lives, so I created a summer basketball day camp for middle school and high school girls. The camp emphasized the growth of the complete person (body, spirit, and mind). I used a lot of the same material that I'd received from the camp I attended while in high school, especially in the area of mental and spiritual growth. There was nothing available like this in the area, so it became open to girls in the outlying schools. The camp was well received, and it began to grow in numbers. I really enjoyed not only coaching the girls but speaking into their spiritual lives as well. Many of them made commitments to God during those years. The only problem for me was that I could not see myself being a high school coach for long. In fact, after a few years, I decided to resign as head coach and pursue other means of helping people.

The local economy began to struggle, which affected the school's funding and the sports teams. We decided to move to a more affluent school district for our children's education and an area that provided more opportunities for my career direction and development. It so happened that we moved closer to both of our families.

We were excited to get started with our family of four in the new area, but moving to the small city did not solve our financial difficulties. We couldn't sell our old house, especially since it was located in such an economically depressed area. We dropped the price of the house way below our purchase price. Even though we eventually sold the house, we lost a substantial amount of money. We began to run up our credit cards. Our financial situation was such that Kathy and I began getting advice from lawyers about pursuing bankruptcy. Kathy began working part-time for a while, but it only paid daycare costs, so we decided it best for her to stay home with our two young children.

Early Marriage And Family

Our indebtedness and the cost of living in this new area led me to begin taking on various part-time jobs in addition to teaching and coaching. Life became busy and stressful. It soon became evident that something had to give. For me, once again, it was my commitment to God. I was still going to church with my family, but honestly, I was not growing in my faith. Church became another thing to do. I enjoyed the feeling I got from attending the Sunday service, but my heart was continually distracted.

My faith took a backseat on my list of priorities. I never intended it to be this way, but it happened. I knew God was with me, and I lived day to day with "good intentions" to make necessary changes in my life that would more directly align with my faith journey (better understanding of God's Word, demonstrating a more Godly love to my wife and children, conquering bad habits, et cetera). I made some halfhearted attempts at changing some of these things, but it seemed like almost immediately I would get busy with one of my jobs and/or the details of raising young children and would resort back to "spiritual survival" mode.

I started writing and singing gospel music with a friend from church. This activity seemed to help my spiritual growth. It focused my mind on things about God, and it was good to have a guy friend with whom I could share my faith. As I think back, I had a lot of male acquaintances who believed as I did, but I never spent much time with them. So now, I was spending time singing with my friend, and it was good. It felt like my spiritual life was finally moving in the right direction. We not only sang together, but talked about our faith, prayed with each other, and shared the joys and struggles of being husbands and fathers.

We soon learned that our music was sounding pretty good. We began to set up concerts and performed publicly. Although the life of a gospel music entertainer provided much needed purpose and enjoyment in my life, it was another thing that took away time from my family. We recorded our music and began selling cassette tapes and CDs at our concerts and, slowly but surely, I was in a business and my fourth job.

Believe me, being a husband, a father of two kids, and working as a teacher and a coach with two additional part-time jobs is not a healthy way to grow spiritually. In fact, it is a good way to burnout completely. Somehow, I made it work for my schedule. But that's the point: everything was part of my schedule, including spending time with my wife and kids. I always justified my use of time with our need for income, trying to work our way out of debt. Life began to center around my jobs as our children entered into school-age.

I convinced myself that I was growing spiritually through the gospel music business, especially since I continued to write songs about God and was able to share the songs and a message of hope with my audiences. The truth is that in my heart there was something missing. I couldn't put my finger on it, but I really believed I still needed a deeper life change. I needed a "spiritual realignment," so to speak. Then something happened that changed the direction of my life forever.

Reflection/Discussion Questions:

1. Humility and self-sacrifice are important virtues in one's spiritual formation. When have you had opportunities to develop and practice these character qualities? Give examples.
2. Has your spiritual life ever taken a backseat? What caused this to happen? Is this what you wanted? How did you respond?
3. Have you ever had a deep sense that something was missing in your life? Can you relate to the phrase "spiritual realignment," or would you call it something else? Explain.
4. Psalm 139:23-24 states, "Search me, God, and know my heart; test me and know my anxious thoughts. See if there is any offensive way in me, and lead me in the way everlasting." Have you ever asked God to do this? How did He respond? Share your story.

OUT OF CONTROL

SICKNESS

Our five-year-old daughter, Melissa, was treated with amoxicillin for a supposed sinus infection and simultaneously came down with a severe case of chicken pox. Although there were not many pox marks, her body was swollen with a spotty red rash, and she ran a 105 degree temperature. She was dehydrated and looked miserable. Time passed, many calls were made to doctors and Melissa showed no signs of improvement. She was losing a lot of energy and looked even sicker. Kathy called the doctor again and was told to go to the hospital to have Melissa seen.

Following an exam, the doctor made it clear that Melissa needed to be transported, preferably by helicopter, to Seattle Children's Hospital, which was 40 minutes away. We were told that her chicken pox was the worst they had seen. Her small body was literally covered with an aggressive red rash.

On that particular evening, a thick fog settled in, and she was not able to be safely transported via helicopter to Seattle. So she was taken to Seattle Children's Hospital by ambulance that night. Kathy went with Melissa. The ambulance sped down the busy roads with its siren blaring. Kathy was thankful for each car that pulled off the road to allow them passage.

Life was spiraling out of control. I began to experience an internal crisis, a deep sense of helplessness. God was becoming more "real" to me than ever before. My prayer life immediately began to change. My conversations with God began to be more frequent and much more desperate.

Melissa arrived safely at the hospital that night, and the doctors began a series of tests on her. It was there in the waiting room that Kathy looked at me with fear in her eyes and said, "I don't think I can go through this." I remember looking at her, offering some words of encouragement, and offering to pray with her. We prayed together that night. This was significant since up to that point in our lives, we had never brought our concerns and cares to God together in prayer. Prayer was always a private activity, except before dinner. During and immediately following the prayer, I recall feeling a peace and confidence that God was in control and that Kathy, our 7-year-old son, and myself were in this for the long haul. Kathy and I had an underlying confidence in the Lord's healing power since we had seen Him take care of Brad as an infant, and He took care of Kathy when she was diagnosed with stage three melanoma cancer the same year. We called our family members and started out the taxing Children's Hospital journey.

Following several days in the hospital and numerous tests, one doctor was able to recognize the difference between the aggressive rash all over Melissa's body and the chicken pox sores. The rash, they discovered, was a reaction to the drug penicillin, which allowed the chicken pox to become aggressive, spreading from her skin to her lungs and eventually into her bone marrow. Her body was disfigured from the swelling of the rash. So disfigured, in fact, that Kathy was asked to bring in a school picture of her to see what she actually looked like. The end result was that she survived, but she had lost two-thirds of her immune system. Melissa now had a very rare immune deficiency. At that time, there was only one other child in the world who had this kind of immune deficiency.

This information brought a lot of questions to Kathy and me: Does she need to live in a sanitary bubble? Can she go to school, church, the store? When she was released from the hospital, she appeared to be very healthy. She participated in all of her outside activities (school, friends, church) and enjoyed a life similar to other 5 and 6 year olds. The only difference was when Melissa caught a common cold, it often immediately turned into pneumonia. During these times Kathy and I had established a routine of patting her upper back intermittently as she breathed in the medicine from a nebulizer. Then she would often be readmitted to Children's Hospital. We became very familiar with the facility and the staff. In fact, at one point, Melissa and Kathy were interviewed on the Seattle Children's Hospital telethon.

Then on February 13th, 1994, the day before Valentine's Day, Kathy noticed a red mark on Melissa's leg. That might sound insignificant, but when your child has a rare immune deficiency, you notice everything new that appears on your child. Melissa went to school that day since it was the last school day before Valentine's Day, and she was adamant about passing out valentines to her friends at school. After school, Melissa was admitted to Children's Hospital again, the 13th time in two years. It was discovered that the red mark on Melissa's leg was an unknown virus. She remained in the hospital and within 24 hours was in the Intensive Care Unit (ICU). She then caught pneumonia, which lengthened her stay. This time she showed very little signs of getting better, because she had developed several more drug allergies over the years. She dropped into a medical coma and barely clung to life. Kathy, myself, and other family members took shifts staying with Melissa, and though she was unresponsive, the equipment indicated that she heard our voices. The small beeps of the heart monitor continued to bring us hope.

Weeks went by with very little improvement. It was obvious that Melissa was a very sick little girl. People from all around were praying for her. I prayed all the time. It seemed like every time I prayed I came away with a peaceful confidence that things would be okay.

Kathy and I got to know other parents in the ICU waiting area. We shared one vital connection with them: the life threatening condition of our children. Each of us could relate to the other. There seemed to be an unspoken understanding of what it means to teeter back and forth from extreme fear to extreme faith. We often spent time talking and praying with each other. Religious differences were overshadowed by the desperation to see our children get better. In those days, the ICU waiting room chairs turned into beds, so in the evening we shared the waiting room with other parents, in a communal style living. Some of the relationships we formed continued for years to follow.

Our community support was amazing! Many employees at the school district where I taught donated hours, so I didn't have to go back to work and our family could be together. We received hundreds of cards and baskets of food from family, friends, and even people we didn't know. In fact, we had only been attending a local church, Mountain View Community Church (MVCC), for about a month and did not know many people there, yet the congregation overwhelmed us with their support. Pastor Matt Knighton, the church's associate pastor, came to the hospital to pray with Melissa and our family. His unselfish compassion and love made a lasting impact on my life. We had many people praying for Melissa and our family. The outpouring of love and generosity from family, friends, and community members was so overwhelming that there were times I shed tears of joy and appreciation.

Submission

One morning, I came back to my mother and father-in-law's home to rest while someone else took the next shift with Melissa at the hospital. As I sat in the bedroom silently and completely exhausted, I can vividly recall the immense feeling of helplessness. Although the doctors assured Kathy and me that they would let us know when the ventilator was not helping, it seemed to me that it really wasn't doing much good, and I became fearful that Melissa's time on earth was getting shorter and shorter. The thought of this brought me to tears. I sat on the side of the bed and wept. Thoughts of life without Melissa ran through my head as sadness flooded me. Then suddenly, I was overwhelmed with a calming Presence. I am convinced it was the presence of God. I began to talk with Him.

I remember looking up and saying, "God, I really don't know you very well at all, but I can't do this alone. I QUIT! I don't quit on you, but I quit on me. I am totally submitting to you. I give you everything. I give you my bad habits, my wife, my house, the hospital bills, the grieving experience, my job. I give you everything.... including Melissa. I don't know what your plan is for her, but I trust you with her. She is your child. She is and will always be a blessing to me, but she is yours. I am weak, Lord. I can't do this. Help me. Help Kathy and I...thank you. I love you, Jesus. If the time has come that you must take Melissa, take care of her. Amen."

I knelt down and fell asleep, exhausted.

The next morning was really no different than any other morning, except I really believed deep down that I'd had a very serious, life changing talk with God. I believed things were going to be different, and I was going to be okay. Following a very difficult month, the doctor told us that the ventilator was not doing anything for Melissa. In fact, he explained to us that she had been on the machine so long at this point that it was actually damaging her lungs. We made the decision to stop the machine. Her time had come. She was already leaving us. Kathy and I stood around her bedside. And soon she was gone. She went to be with Jesus, as we sang, "Jesus Loves Me."

Following a lot of hugs and tears, we walked down the lonely hospital halls. As we walked, Kathy asked me if we should try to have another child. We were in our late thirties and having children was not easy for us. Neither of us wanted to go through this pain again, but we both agreed that we would place our trust in God and try to have another child. We gave our son Brad a hug and together, with other family members, we left the hospital.

Reflection/Discussion Questions:

1. Has there been a time in your life that everything seemed to be out of control? How did you respond? What was your relationship with God like during this time in your life? Is it different now? Share your experience.

2. Have you ever turned everything over to God? What does submission mean to you? Share your story.
3. John 14:1 states, "Do not let your hearts be troubled. You believe in God; believe also in me." How does this verse speak to you at this time in your life?

GRIEVING, SPIRITUAL FORMATION, AND RECOVERY

LIFE AFTER DEATH

The moment Melissa died, it was like part of me died as well. It seems like I bypassed the standard stages of grief (shock, denial, and bargaining) and dove straight to depression. The cloud was dark and dense. Although it hovered over me for months, I never lost the idea that things would be okay. My faith in God was ever present. I would often sit alone, with that cloud lingering over my head while reading Scripture or my devotions. I would sometimes record my experiences, thoughts, and feelings in a journal, reflecting in times of severe pain, extreme hope, desperation and security, turmoil and peace.

I spent hours staring at trees and listening to the wind as it whistled though the tall grass and treetops. I talked a lot with God during these times. I don't recall what I talked about. I don't recall being angry, but I do remember asking Him some very personal questions, like I was talking to a friend. I would ask, "Lord God, where did you take Melissa? Is this what life is about, live for a short time, then go to be with you?" Life is so short. At times I would even make desperate attempts to talk with Melissa. I would tearfully cry out words like, "Hi, Melissa, take care of Grandma okay? I'm still singin' songs down here. I sure miss you, but I know Jesus is taking care of you." The conversations were painful, and they often induced a flood of tears. Then the tears would stop, and I would move on to something else. This went on for months. It was always a painful process, yet it was a cleansing process as well. It was like I stood helplessly before God exposing my open wound and trusting Him, the Great Physician, to heal and restore me. I had nothing to hide. I was lying on the operating table of life, chest open and heart exposed, dying so it seemed, and trusting God with my life.

As a school teacher, I always looked forward to the summer months. The summer after Melissa died I was especially looking forward to spending time fishing. I actually enjoy catching fish, though this particular summer it really had very little to do with the act of fishing itself. I often found myself going to a local fishing dock. Many times I would throw my fishing line into the lake and stare at the clouds and listen to the laughter of children in the background. I would smell the rich, comforting fragrance of the early morning lake as I watched the ducks and listened to the wind whisper through the trees. It was like I was sitting there emptying my heart and soul and allowing God to fill it with His comforting Spirit. I guess you could say I was grieving or meditating, or depressed. I really don't know. I sure didn't take the time and energy to psychoanalyze myself. I was at the lake, on a dock, and it seemed that God was present, and I needed Him. You see, during that season in my life, I needed to simply be with Him; and for me there is no better place for that than by a lake or in any serene natural environment.

Frequently, an elderly man would join me on the dock. He would stand across from me and throw his line into the water and fish. I like to tell people that we had many deep theological discussions and that is the reason he is part of my spiritual journey, but that is not true. The fact is that the man said very few words. In fact, the only thing I recall about our conversation was his question,

"What ya' usin'?" and my response being, "Power bait or worms." That is about as deep as the conversation went.

This man was quite a bit older than me, dressed in very grubby fishing clothes, and had a face that represented former, or possibly current, pain and suffering. His face was tattered and worn, and his teeth were nearly black from tobacco use, I assume. He wore an old, dirty fishing cap and bib overalls that had seen better days. He didn't have anything to say, probably because he really didn't have anything to say. But his company on the dock was helpful to me simply because he was there during an extremely difficult time in my life.

His presence was comforting to me because honestly, it seemed like he had been through sorrow. I never asked him, but it appeared as though he had seen hard times throughout his life, and it was good to know that I wasn't alone in my deep misery and grief. I wasn't sure I would even survive. I appreciated that he didn't offer insight, comfort, advice, or even encouragement. I could relate to the old saying, "Silence is golden."

God uses people for our spiritual growth in many ways, and quite often it is not the words we speak that influences our lives, but instead merely being alongside them. Let's face it, we often talk too much. There are definitely times for positive input, good counsel, and sound advice, but I discovered that there are also times to be quiet in God's presence and listen to His still small voice, allowing Him to speak deeply into my soul.

My wife, Kathy, was dealing with her own grief and was also pregnant at the time, so she was not feeling up to doing very much at all, especially fishing. Our 10-year-old son, Brad, on the other hand, enjoyed going to the lake. We spent many hours fishing that summer, sometimes from the dock, sometimes in the canoe, or with my brother in his motorized boat. We caught a lot of fish that summer, but most importantly we created stories together, and we were there for each other through months of grieving. We never talked much about Melissa's death, or grieving, but the mere act of being together, especially at the lake seemed to help me take steps toward recovery.

Reflection/Discussion Questions

1. Have you ever experienced a significant loss (death of a loved one, friend, job, identity, dream, or divorce)? Describe your feelings and behavior immediately after the loss.
2. Have you ever found it helpful to spend time alone with God? Explain.

3. Have you ever had someone's quiet presence be a comforting experience for you? Share your experience.

Reentry troubles

I understand now that there are various stages we go through when grieving, but during the first year following Melissa's death, I didn't know much at all about the stages of grief. All I really knew was that I hurt a lot, so did my wife, my son, and our families. The emotions I felt were different every day. Actually, they were different every hour...or even every 15 minutes. My wife and I warned each other when a "wave" was coming, which meant we were about to be washed away with an emotion. We would brace ourselves for the wave and ride it out. Sometimes we would hug each other and cry. There was often nothing obvious that had triggered the emotion. It would just show up, out of nowhere, and life would stop for a few minutes as we would ride out the wave.

I often felt extreme numbness in public places. It seemed like everyone was walking in slow motion. During times like these, I had no control over the strange and unpleasant emotions inside of me.

Even if others are present, grief is a lonely walk in the dark. Although it did help to attend a few grief support group sessions, I continued to have bouts of loneliness and depression. No matter who I talked with, it seemed like no one really understood; and for reasons that escaped me, I desperately needed to be understood. Many caring, loving people tried their best to walk with me through this time, yet I still felt alone.

The strangest part was it didn't even feel like my wife understood. This now makes more sense to me because, as I learned years later, each of us grieves differently. We really didn't share our feelings until years later. We struggled to communicate honestly about how we felt. We held so much hurt and didn't know what to do with it. Let's face it, couples are statistically at a greater risk of separation after the loss of a child. Well, I can testify that Kathy and I had our share of problems, but I can also assure you that by the grace of God, the power of love, and the commitment to each other and family, we stayed together. We are both thankful for the many ways our new church family helped us not to feel so lost as we navigated through these dark times.

I don't recall specifically when it happened, but there was a time in my grieving that I remembered the commitment I had made to the Lord prior to Melissa's death. I had promised to give God everything. I had told Him that I would give up myself and was willing to allow Him to truly be my Lord.

I had a strong desire to know God. I wanted to be His friend and possibly even His servant or minister. I started reading Scripture , Christian books, commentaries, and books on grieving.. I began to journal. I wrote thoughts, poems, ideas, questions, prayers, and anything that came to mind. And I prayed all the time…literally all time.

God walked with me everywhere I went. My prayers were endless conversations with my friend and Lord, Jesus. The more this continued, the less alone I felt. Oh sure, people still didn't understand what I was going through, but that was manageable now. I came to realize that others will probably never completely understand. God and I were developing an authentic relationship, and it was refreshing. He understood. I felt less isolated, and my wife and son, in their own ways, were showing similar changes.

Although I began to feel like I was able to gradually move forward, there were still troubles as I reentered the world. The most basic activities became triggers. Even going to the grocery store was difficult. A trip down the cereal aisle would elicit the "wave" as I recalled Melissa begging for attention. I remember thinking, "Wow! I can't even get through a grocery store."

I even had trouble watching cartoons or listening to Disney songs. Melissa loved the music from some of the popular Disney movies showing at the time (i.e.

"Aladdin" and "Lion King"). When I heard specific songs like "Whole New World", the "wave" would appear and life stopped – sometimes for a moment and sometimes longer. There were so many of these "reentry trouble spots" that I lost count.

During this stage of grieving, everything was related to Melissa. I couldn't even escape the pain when I slept. I would have dreams about times spent with Melissa. In fact, on more than one occasion my mind would play tricks on me as I would hear familiar "Melissa" noises coming from her bedroom or in the living room. I started to question my sanity, but when I told Kathy, she in fact, shared some of her similar experiences, which helped me realize how powerful grief can be.

God and I had many, many conversations during these times. I continually filled my mind with "God thoughts" through Scripture and devotional readings.

All in all, I appeared to be moving forward through the initial grieving process, though it seemed to last forever. But there was an event that was very significant in helping me to heal even further.

This was the day that I cleaned out Melissa's bedroom. Months had passed since Melissa's death, and Kathy and I had avoided going into her bedroom. There is something special about a 7-year-old girl's bedroom. Everything seemed to be special to Melissa: her clothes, her toys, her music, bracelets, art projects, books, all were her "very special" things. The thought of facing this task was horrific. Thinking of getting rid of these things was worse than horrific it was terrifying, but it needed to be done.

One Saturday, when Kathy and our son Brad were not at home, I ventured into Melissa's room and began placing her things into boxes in preparation for giving them away. The experience was just like I had anticipated. Horrific. Every single item I picked up triggered a flashback of times spent with Melissa. I cried continually for the entire time that I was boxing up her things. In the middle of the tears, I would cry out to God to help me. This went on and on until the job was finished. The tears gradually subsided. I was exhausted, but knew I had accomplished something significant and could now move on. Kathy donated most of Melissa's items to children in crises. Melissa would have liked that.

Finally, I felt ready to return to work. I was a middle school teacher, and the students were ready for me to come back to class, though I was not one hundred percent prepared for them. Honestly, the thought of facing hormonally charged 12-14 year olds was nerve wracking. But as it happened, the transition went well. The students were gracious and kind, and I was grateful for their restraint in asking questions about Melissa's death.

I appreciated how the school counselor, the teachers, and principal had helped prepare them for my arrival.

At the end of the school year, our entire school of approximately 200 students went to a roller skating rink to celebrate. It sounded like a lot of fun, but as I arrived I was confronted with another "reentry" issue: the "wave" suddenly emerged. I thought I had been making progress in my grieving. In fact, I had thought I was done. How wrong I was! That skating rink was the same facility in which Melissa had taken skating lessons a year before her passing. The smells and the surrounding sights were too much for me.

I asked the school counselor to take charge of my class; and I got in the car and cried all the way home. Reentering into society was going to take a lot longer than I had expected. There were going to be more rough roads ahead. I told myself that I didn't have an option, I had to engage with life: reenter into work, the grocery store, community events, and society. But I couldn't do this alone.

I once again had some very intimate conversations with God. I found myself often driving to a local trailhead and sitting there for extended periods of time, reading Scripture, journaling, and praying.

The Lord started planting a thought in my head: If I really was committed to Him, I must have a better understanding of Him, trust Him more, and obey Him more implicitly. The thought of this idea was a bit uncomfortable for me because it was the truth staring me right in the face. I was doing all right with God when I needed comfort, hope, and peace, but as soon as I sensed that He wanted me to more fully trust and obey Him, I became uneasy. Why? Because obedience is a difficult road. Although it was going to be a long hard path, I really sensed it was time for me to up my commitment to God.

REFLECTION/DISCUSSION QUESTIONS:

1. Have you ever had similar experiences with either the "wave" or numbness? Tell about it.
2. Do you think it is important to have faith in God during a time of loss? Why or why not?
3. Give examples of "reentry troubles" you have experienced in your life.
4. Do you think God wants us to understand Him better, trust Him, and obey Him?
5. Isaiah 41:10 states, "So do not fear, for I am with you; do not be dismayed, for I am your God. I will strengthen you, and I will help you; I will uphold you with my righteous right hand." Which part of this verse comforts you the most? Explain.

MOVING FORWARD

MAKING CHANGES

*I*t would appear that I was doing pretty well in the "commitment to God" department. I was going to church regularly. I prayed and wrote songs about God and regularly pointed people to Him. What else did I need to do? Well, the Spirit strongly impressed upon me that in order for me to really commit myself to Him, I first needed to intentionally and strategically build a more personal relationship with Him. So I began to read, study, and deeply contemplate the Bible more than ever I had. I tried to get as much as I could out of the Sunday teachings. And of course I kept my conversations with God alive and authentic.

It turns out my wife and son were doing the same things in their own lives. Kathy was experiencing her own life changes. She sat for hours at Melissa's gravesite alone, pregnant, and praying to God. She often carried her Bible to the site and dove deep into Scripture as she dealt with her anger and convictions. In fact, it was during one of these gravesite visits that she came to a personal saving faith.

I was also convicted that if I was to be the Lord's authentic and effective disciple, I must change some of my secret habits and coping behaviors. I came to a place that I honestly believed I needed to make changes in my life, not for the purpose of looking like a "good Christian," but because in my soul I sincerely wanted to grow closer to God and didn't want anything to get in the way. I wanted to know Him in a new, richer way, and it seemed like some of my habits were preventing that from happening. This passion began a very long, intentional process of personal change and spiritual growth.

I began my transformation by being honest about my consumption of alcohol. I concluded that I drank not because I liked the taste, which is how I always had justified it, but simply for the numbing effect. Although I had not gone to any drinking parties or taverns with the purpose of getting drunk for many years, I was routinely drinking a few beers, particularly at the end of the day to help me relax. Well, quite often, the few beers became more. All this to say, I committed myself to stop using alcohol. I told myself that I was going to try to stop drinking through a process of abstinence, prayer, and journaling. If that was not helpful, I was going to use the 12-step process from AA. I was very serious about quitting completely. I am thankful that since that day I have not consumed alcohol.

It was during this time that Kathy stopped drinking alcohol as well. Being pregnant provided good incentive, but in the process of abstinence, she recognized an unhealthy, ongoing desire to drink alcohol, so she decided to permanently stop.

Now granted, I am not legalistic about Christians using alcohol, but I reasoned with myself that if I was going to be a more effective witness and a disciple of Christ, I needed to stop using substances to get a buzz. I believed that this was not how Jesus reacted to the stress of life. Besides, I was very aware that I have a family history of alcoholism, which concerned me. Also there were a few times in college that people confronted me about my excessive drinking and challenged me to get help – advice that I ignored at the time.

During this time in my life, I was also convicted about my use of tobacco and my lustful thinking. The decision to not use tobacco was not a moral decision but more because it was an addiction that I had carried with me for many years. I had used chewing tobacco since I was in the 5th grade. Granted, there were many times that I had tried to quit, but had never seemed to be able to kick the habit. I think I had tried to quit about 20 times over the years. Once again, I had trouble picturing my Lord Jesus with a pinch of tobacco in his mouth as a way to relieve stress or to celebrate victories for that matter. It took a few months, but I am very grateful that I finally am able to live my life tobacco free.

My decision to deal with lustful thinking on the other hand was a moral decision. The Bible is very clear about what God thinks about sexual sin and a lustful heart. I knew deep down that even though I was happily married, at times my heart was not pure. When being honest with myself, I could see how the sexual sins of my past affected my heart in the present, and I believed that I must make some serious changes if I was to really grow spiritually.

I developed a burning desire to be a witness and disciple of Jesus, which meant changes were still needed. I became more focused on spiritual concerns and more intentional in my approach to life. This became a challenge. There were many internal conflicts along the way. I discovered that throughout the years, I had formed certain beliefs that directly and indirectly impacted my thinking and behavior. For example, since my childhood, I had carried with me the belief that my worth as a person was based on performance. This is a false belief. It is a lie. I can give many examples of how this negatively influenced my thinking and behaviors growing up. Throughout the years, I learned certain performance strategies and how to manipulate people and life in order to get what I ultimately desired, significance. This manipulating behavior, I discovered, was damaging to me and others.

I gradually came to realize that much of my thinking, belief systems, and world views needed some serious modifications. I knew that in order to experience this level of change, I had to get to the root of my beliefs. I was well aware that this kind of personal transformation was going to take hard work, time, and the power of God's activity in my life. It wasn't going to be a quick fix as a result of reading a few motivational books or listening to great speakers.

I began to grow in my knowledge of God, develop a biblical worldview, and gain a better understanding of basic biblical doctrines through the teachings and guidance I received at MVCC, my church, under the leadership of Pastor Roland Classen. I was mentored by Pastor Roland. He spent many hours investing in my spiritual growth through teaching, counseling, listening, praying, and directing me, and I am forever grateful. I was also mentored by Mountain View's associate pastor, Matt Knighton. Matt and I had many breakfast meetings together where he allowed me to sort out my thinking and beliefs at the time and provided me with much needed spiritual insight. Roland and Matt continue to be an important part of my life to this day.

I also participated in a course that Pastor Matt led. It taught effective ways to share God's love and hope with people. It was valuable to me at the time because I was falling more and more in love with Jesus and less and less in love with the ways of the world. I wanted everyone to know about the hope they can have in God if they allow Him to really live in and throughout their lives. The class helped equip me in sharing this hope with others.

Kathy and I had another child, Jacob, about this time. He was born exactly nine months to the day from when we buried Melissa. Our son was born a month early because he entered the world in a state of crisis. His umbilical cord was wrapped around his neck three times. This crisis was not what Kathy and I needed following the loss of Melissa, but as it turns out it was another reminder that we are not the ones in control, and it gave us another opportunity to place our trust in God.

A new child in our home provided us much joy and life. It was around this time that I was inspired to write children's songs. I produced a few kids' CDs and developed a storytelling character I called Mr. Maker, based on a story I used to tell Brad and Melissa when they were young. I began sharing music and stories with children at school assemblies, preschools, state fairs, and birthday parties. This creative outlet was rewarding, and my connection with young children provided healing and a purpose for me. It continues to be an avenue of joy and direction as I share music with hurting children and families at Seattle Children's Hospital.

I used my music and storytelling to share the message of God's love and hope. When Jacob was in diapers, he would come with me as I ministered at summer camps, backyard Bible clubs, and nursing homes. In fact, at one point our whole family (Kathy, myself, Brad – now in high school – and Jacob) traveled around and ministered at summer camps. I led worship and spoke to the campers while Kathy provided creative Bible stories. Brad served as a counselor, and Jacob did his thing as a typical 5 year old set free to experience the joys of nature, running, climbing trees, building forts, and hanging out with campers. God used each of us to care for people as we related our life story. We enjoyed meeting many believers throughout the Pacific Northwest. Several of them became lifelong friends.

Those early ministry years had a valuable impact on my spiritual formation. It was an opportunity to serve the Lord as a family, an opportunity to really begin thinking through my biblical understanding and convictions as I prepared the songs and messages for the campers. It was an opportunity to be blessed by some wonderful campers and camp staff, and it was an important part of my calling into ministry. It was around this time that I chose to let go of full-time teaching, which I had done for over 20 years, and pursue Christian ministry as a vocation.

Part of a person's spiritual formation will inevitably involve helping other people. It has certainly been true for me. It is similar to the grieving process. Many months after Melissa died, I had a tremendous longing to share God's love with people, specifically those who were experiencing pain, loneliness, and depression. I wanted to bring His light to people living in the darkness that I had experienced.

I first shared with the residents at a nursing facility primarily for head trauma patients. I went there to sing with the goal of sharing God's love and His message of hope with hurting people. It was around Christmas time, and I had practiced some Christmas songs on my guitar. When I entered the facility, there were only five patients as my audience.

I began to sing, and then was interrupted by a man yelling from his wheelchair and waving his arms. I stopped and asked him what he wanted. He yelled, "Play 'Achy Breaky Heart'!" This surprised me a bit since I was not prepared to be interrupted and to be asked to play a song unrelated to God. Well, I thought about the melody for a few minutes and then began to sing the chorus of "Achy Breaky Heart." The five patients smiled, clapped their hands, and attempted to sing along.

Something happened at that moment: God was using the patients to teach me spiritual truths about how to love, and how to be filled with joy, especially when hurting. God was teaching me humility. I was seeing the importance of setting aside my pride and being authentic with people. I was beginning to grasp the idea that life was actually not about me. The folks at this nursing facility became friends of mine from that day on. I am in continual contact with these people and have provided a chapel service for the residents every month since that day.

In time, I chose to formalize my Bible education and pastoral training. I began taking Bible courses as I pursued the ordination process with the Christian and Missionary Alliance (C&MA). At the same time, I continued to teach school part-time and serve part-time at the church.

Gradually, I completed my academic studies, became an ordained Pastor with the C&MA, and began ministering more at MVCC. Following a formalized Clinical Pastoral Education process with HCMA (Healthcare Chaplains Ministry Association), I began serving as a local healthcare chaplain. Then a few years later, I completed a formal education in biblical counseling with the American Association of Christian Counselors at Light University and gradually became certified as a pastoral counselor through them.

I spent hours upon hours (and still do) ministering to hurting people through care and counseling ministries at the local church and in various healthcare settings. Also, I make weekly visits to the Seattle Children's Hospital where I provide harmonica and ukulele music to the patients, families, and staff.

It has been my experience that as we commit our lives to God, He truly does provide the way. He uses our talents, personality, and life experiences (good and bad) for His purposes. And through Him the painful, emptiness deep in our hearts is not only filled, but it becomes fuel for even greater service.

Reflection/Discussion Questions:

1. Have you ever had a passion to really get to know God? What did you do? How did you pursue Him? What does it mean to trust and obey God?
2. Have you ever felt a conviction to eliminate "secret habits" that are barriers to knowing and experiencing God? If so, what did you do with this conviction?

Moving Forward

3. Proverbs 3:5-6 says, "Trust in the L ORD with all of your heart and lean not on your own understanding. In all your ways acknowledge Him, and He will make your paths straight." Has this been true in your life? Explain.
4. Do you agree that God uses all our talents, personality traits, and life experiences (good and bad) for His purposes? Explain.

BUMPS IN THE ROAD

DARK CLOUDS

Although I was experiencing tremendous growth in understanding myself, God, and others, I was not void of temptation, spiritual warfare, and more internal troubles to confront. I learned that this process would be a lifelong endeavor. It happened when I was elbow deep in ministry – a couple of dark clouds from my past began to surface.

I was serving in a pastoral care position at the church, ministering as a healthcare chaplain, and walking alongside many hurting people. Kathy and I were also spending a lot of time with a couple of individuals who were dying. I was emotionally drained. Believe me, Satan knows our weaknesses. Some dark clouds of my past began to gather again. These dark clouds could be summarized as pride (I am more special/I can do it alone) and lust (obsessive desire and want). Two areas I had thought were completely dealt with and didn't need to be addressed anymore had cropped back up in my life.

I soon realized the opposite is true. I discovered that the more I grew in my spiritual health and commitment to the Lord's service, the more battles I would face. There really is such a thing as spiritual warfare, and though I don't completely understand how it all works, I can verify that it is real.

I began to feel spiritually dead, even though I was fervently praying to God, confessing my sins, and making every effort to emerge victorious from the fight.

I felt stuck and unable to change. My behavior gave clear evidence of a developing spiritual disease, and I knew it could ruin my life. Then one night, I made a commitment to God and myself to confront the enemy of my soul and really deal with pride and lust. It was through His loving and prodding Spirit that I finally came to the place of wanting Him to make a deeper level of change in my life.

After an honest and open talk with my wife, I contacted a Christian counselor in hopes of moving forward toward greater spiritual health. So it is that I began to reveal a world of hidden wounds and repressed feelings to the counselor. After a couple sessions, he suggested that I go to some men's small groups. Reluctantly I agreed. I also began working through a Christian 12-step program and soon learned that at the core of my being were a series of character flaws that I had never admitted and most certainly had never addressed.

I needed other men in my life, not only for accountability, but accessibility. I needed authentic male relationships. It didn't even occur to me how lonely and isolated my life had become and how much pain and resentment I was carrying around. I had mastered the art of denial and was skilled in avoiding conflict and sweeping uncomfortable realities under the carpet.

It became obvious that I had serious issues with making sure I didn't upset people. It was like my worth as a human being was dependant on how well I smoothed over problems and appeared to be in control. This created "under the surface" anxiety. I had spent years developing "image management." You know, looking in control, looking good, looking right, looking spiritual, and looking intelligent. The truth is that I had been struggling with pride all of my life.

I also came to realize that I had been struggling with lust most of my life. I discovered how it was deeply hidden in my heart, going back to my preadolescent years. It is relatively easy to recognize lust when engaged in various forms of sexual lust (something very prevalent during my early years), but it is not as obvious when lust presents ially acceptable ways (the lust to be valued, attractive, respected). I saw in how a lustful heart is very deceptive and decay and spiritual turmoil.

I honestly didn't like what I discovered as I began working through some of these issues. I knew what God thought about pride and lust. Scripture makes it clear. No wonder my spiritual life had been stagnant.

So, I continued the painful, time-intensive work of personal change. The more I learned about myself and allowed God's Spirit to use my wife, pastors, loyal friends, other broken and redeemed men, the 12-step process, and God's Word, the more I began to see real change in my heart.

I can't overemphasize the level of intentional, ongoing openness to correction and the willingness to experience spiritual growing pains as necessary to begin seeing fruit in one's life. At least, it was that way for me. It seems like so many of us want results immediately and thus give up when the desired outcome isn't experienced immediately. God has His own timetable, and we must be continually obedient to His Spirit and place our trust in Him and His timing.

At the time, I was ministering at a local gospel mission, and I was working with the mission's recovery program. In order to do this, I had to go through their relapse prevention training. Well, the timing could not have been better (Isn't that just like God!). The training was very comprehensive and extremely practical. This required me to work through my own issues, and in the process, I became more spiritually grounded and healthy.

Through the long, painful process of change I began to develop a grateful heart. Gratitude and thankfulness are extremely important to personal health and recovery. I found myself spending more time in solitude, seeking God, praying, and reflecting on the small gifts God had provided for me. I spent hours seeking God as I sat by a lake, writing, listening, watching wildlife, and enjoying the sounds of children playing in the sand and the water. I often brought my ukulele and harmonica to the beach and played melodies as I let God take a hold of my mind and heart. I continue this practice to this day. God once again had a way of providing me with exactly what I needed.

My spiritual growth and recovery continues today. I learn and grow every day. I'm a work in progress. One day at a time I interact with God, enjoy His creation, and build relationships; and through the process of living each day, I grow, and I change. I'm growing and, by God's grace, becoming more like Jesus, my Lord. I don't completely understand how this growing and changing thing actually works, but I do know that it is important that I stay the course and keep in step with God's Spirit as He guides me along the way.

Reflection/Discussion Questions:

1. Do you believe there is such a thing as "spiritual warfare"? Do you think you have ever experienced it? Explain.
2. Have you ever had dark clouds from your past rise up during a time when you thought things were going well? Describe your experience.
3. A grateful heart is an important part of spiritual health and recovery. Do you have a grateful heart? What makes it grateful or not?
4. Do you agree that the process of substantial, long-term change involves staying the course and keeping in step with God's Spirit?
5. Romans 12:2 states, "Do not conform any longer to the pattern of this world, but be transformed by the renewing of your mind." How would you apply this verse? Give examples.

HUNGER AND THIRST

JOURNEY WITH GRATITUDE

I cherish quiet times with God. Throughout the years, I have discovered many special places to be alone with Him. During the winter, I enjoy sitting in a dark room next to a candle or small light. Yet, I enjoy sitting next to a window listening to the birds during the springtime. But it is summertime and late autumn when I frequently spend time alone with God in the quietness of the outdoors, allowing Him to speak into my spirit as I listen to His still small voice. Often such times have inspired me to write poems and song lyrics that express the deepest thoughts of my inner world. I encourage you to authentically seek after God and find a special place to simply "be" with God.

Many people have told me they don't have time for this. I ask them if they have time to eat, and of course they eat. So I remind them to think about these things as spiritual meals. If you are like many people, there is a good chance you are spiritually malnourished. I know, because I was for years.

Here are a couple of the poetic verses I have written during these quiet times with God. They each reflect the theme of gratitude, a vital component in every healthy spiritual life. These are taken from my booklet, "Journey with Gratitude." I hope these thoughts can be a source of encouragement to you as you progress on your own spiritual journey.

TODAY I AM GRATEFUL
I'm stuck in a rut
Again,
But
I won't give up...
So I face the wind,
The pain, the fear...
And I
spread my wings
and lift my head
and
soar
again!
PAUSE AND PRAY

Another excerpt from my "Journey with Gratitude" booklet:

TODAY I AM GRATEFUL

A trail of

dried tears...

A pathway

to

peace

PAUSE and PRAY

WHAT DOES IT MEAN?

QUESTIONS FROM "INSIDE OF RECOVERING HEARTS":

*I*n many ways, the content of this book reflects the spirituality lecture I have presented to patients for many years. As a part of this lecture I often leave time for discussion. This section will describe the many interactions I have had with patients' over the years and gives examples of the discussions we have.

Discussion Question: What does it mean to turn control over to your "higher power"? (A term commonly used in 12-Step programs defined as a power/supreme being or deity, greater than our self)

Patient Response: It means to "let go and let God" or to give your worries to your higher power. It is important to make a decision and leave the result with God.

My Response: Turning control over to God is an act of submission. When I looked to God, prior to my daughter's death, and said, "I quit," I was truly giving all control over to Him. Deep down, I knew I could not do life without God in control. I had to admit that I was completely powerless and He was all powerful. Turning control over to God is humbling.

I first turned control over to God at the basketball camp when I was in high school, and again when I recommitted myself to God following a lengthy season of self-centered disobedience.

It has been my experience and the experience of many others that turning control over to God is NOT a onetime event. It has been my experience that we must continually turn our lives over to God. It is a lifestyle, an ongoing, daily experience.

Discussion Question: When people turn control over to their "higher power" they often speak of a new sense of freedom. What does freedom mean?

Patient Response: You become free of your burdens or free of your worries. One becomes free of themselves.

What Does It Mean?

My Response: As a Christian, I recognize that the Bible teaches us that believing, receiving, and abiding in Jesus sets us free. We are free from sin's controlling power and free to live in peace, now and for eternity (Colossians 1:21-22).

(At the recovery center I often elaborate on what "freedom" can look like.)

The opposite of freedom is bondage. Bondage can be pictured as being tied to a stake that is buried deep in the ground and connected to an extremely strong bungi cord. The strong bungi cord, as strong as it is, has enough flexibility to allow for some movement on our part. This illustrates how we "stretch the limits" of the cord (sin) that binds us. Although we are bound by the cord and the stake, we persistently make every attempt to stretch or push the limits to justify and/or minimize our selfish, sinful ways. We try harder and harder to live in a kind of "false freedom" while still connected to our selfishness and sin. We try to live in freedom on our terms but the cord only stretches for a while, then it snaps us back to reality (bondage). Sound familiar?

Freedom occurs when the bungi cord is cut. SNAP... FREEDOM. This creates a freedom to be truly free and to live without enslavement.

My Christian faith points me to the Scriptures, which tells us that we were once enslaved (bound) to sin and darkness but now we are not (Galatians 5:1). We now have other options. We become free to choose a different route, a different path. At one time we were unable to do this for we were slaves to our old selves. But freedom in Christ allows us to choose life instead of death, light instead of darkness (Galatians 5:16-25).

We soon discover that living in freedom is not easy. We need God, and we need others. We were created for relationships, and it is through relationships (God and others) we learn how to live in freedom.

Patient Question: I have been advised to do the 12-step program, which means you must believe in a higher power. I have had no indoctrination regarding spiritual things (no church, Sunday school, youth group, temple), so what am I supposed to do for this part of my recovery?

My Response: Begin with a simple, honest prayer.

Patient Response: Is it ok to pray if you don't know who you are praying to?

My Response: When I first heard that question it silenced me for a moment, and I thought to myself "good question."

What Does It Mean?

Then I recalled the story from the Scriptures when Jesus brought a small child onto His lap and said, "Let the little children come to me, and do not hinder them, for the kingdom of God belongs to such as these. Truly I tell you, anyone who will not receive the kingdom of God like a little child will never enter it" (Mark 10:14-15). These are powerful words. He is telling us that we should approach Him like a young child, who has faith and trusts without a second thought.

It immediately occurred to me how I have witnessed many children praying to God. They pray with enthusiasm, with sincerity, and with faith. Do these little kids have a theological education? Do they really know theologically who God is? Of course not, and yet they pray and God listens. So you can pray if you don't know the specifics of who you are praying to. Just pray, begin the initial conversation like you are talking to a person you haven't met, someone who wants to be your friend, Savior, God, and life companion. We are created with a "God vacuum" in our hearts, which is why it is so natural for most people to pray. So simply do what comes more naturally than you might think.

Patient Question: I was once really spiritual. I went to church all the time. I was really connected with God, but now I have lost it. How can I get my spiritual life back on track?

My Response: Do you recall my prayer to God prior to my daughter's death? I said, "God, I don't really even know who you are, but I can't do this alone." The reality is that even though I asked God into my life in the later part of my high school years, and I returned to Him following a time of rebellion, I still had to admit that I didn't really know Him very well at all. It is so important to come to God anyway as you understand Him at that point in time. As you continue your pursuit of Him, your understanding will grow.

Although God doesn't change, we do. As we seek, we will grow throughout our life. We will make connections with God differently. Therefore, don't stop seeking!

It is important to remember that even though we change as we journey through different seasons of life, God does NOT change. He is always there. If you had a relationship with God throughout your childhood, but seem to be "losing it" now, I suggest that you go back to the basics: PRAY! Tell God about your confusion. Tell Him about your desire to be reacquainted with Him. Pray. Talk with Him. Listen to Him. You may need to spend some time asking for forgiveness. And trust Him that He

What Does It Mean?

truly is faithful in forgiving your sins. Remember God is about new beginnings. Pray.

Patient Question: How do you pray? Are there other ways that communication can take place between you and God?

My Response: There are numerous ways we can communicate with God. First there is prayer. But prayer is basically talking and listening to God, sometimes using words, and other times not using words.

This definition seems to be a bit too simple for some people, so I will remind you that you actually pray every day at the recovery center. The Serenity Prayer, a prayer that is routinely repeated after group meetings, is a very popular and an often quoted prayer in recovery circles. If the only thing you get out of your 21 day experience is the Serenity Prayer, than you have received a great start … if you believe the words that it proclaims! There is so much truth in the words of the prayer, and remember <u>God</u> is in control, not us.

> "God grant me
> the Serenity
> to accept the things

> I cannot change,
> the courage
> to change the things
> I can and
> the wisdom
> to know the difference."
> Reinhold Niebuhr

This is a liturgical prayer. It is a prayer written out and intended to be read, and there are many, many great prayers of this nature, for example, the Lord's Prayer in Matthew 6:9-13.

What are the benefits and disadvantages of this kind of prayer?

The advantage of this kind of prayer is that through the process of reading it routinely, it will penetrate deep into the memory and ultimately the heart of the person. The disadvantage of this is that it can lose its meaning. People repeat prayers so often that they actually forget what they are repeating. Truth and passion become mere words. That is why the Serenity Prayer is an excellent prayer ... if you BELIEVE it.

Don't try to over think your prayer life. Keep it simple, either talk to God, as a loving, caring Father, or read the prayer one word or phrase at a time. Focus on the truth of the words. Meditate upon the meaning.

What Does It Mean?

There are also many other ways to communicate with God: acts of kindness, journaling, silent meditation or contemplative prayer, and the arts (music, painting, dance).

The point is that there are many ways people communicate with God. Don't limit yourself to sitting by your bedside with your hands folded and saying a proper sounding prayer.

Keep your communication line open spontaneously, naturally, and continuously.

It is also very important to periodically stop talking and intentionally listen. I found that quite often my part in communing with God is being quiet. Scripture reminds me, in facing the greatness of God, Job realized that he needed to stop talking and just listen to the wisdom of God. I remember learning this through my quiet days on the fishing dock months after my daughter, Melissa, died. I spent hours saying nothing, but it seemed like God was communicating with me. This act represents a kind of contemplative/reflective prayer. It involves silence and listening, which is a lot more difficult than it seems. You communicate with your entire being (body, spirit, soul) by the mere discipline of being silent. I don't claim to completely understand this, but I can tell you that when deep in your heart you are seeking God, and you shut your mouth and listen to Him, He will meet you. Whether you understand what He is saying or not isn't the point.

The point is that God and you met, and a lot can happen after that.

Patient Question: Prior to asking the question the patient told a personal story. He shared that his uncle loved God very much. In fact he was a committed and a faithful servant of God. He was very ill and in the hospital for a long time. He had suffered a lot. One time during his hospitalization, he repeatedly told his nephew that God was going to heal him. He told him to keep his head up and know for certain that God was going to heal him. That was very encouraging indeed, but there came a time when the boy's uncle became increasingly ill and eventually died.

The patient looked at me and asked with an angry tone: "You keep talking about God. I have gone through a tremendous amount of suffering and have seen a lot of suffering and pain. Where is this God you keep talking about?"

My Response: Of course the room got very quiet and all eyes were looking at me. I paused for a moment, turned to the man and asked, "May I ask you a question?"

"Yes," he replied.

I asked, "Do you believe your uncle is healed now?" He looked up and shook his head in agreement.

I continued, "Then would you say your uncle was wrong or right in stating that God was going to heal him?"

The patients at the recovery center sat in silence as the man said that his uncle was accurate in saying that God was going to heal him. He was at peace with that answer.

I then looked toward the group and reminded them that all of us have a serious problem, one that we must candidly acknowledge and carefully address: control. We want to call the shots.

The problem is so huge that we even try to control God. We have a tendency to put God in a box, and if He doesn't meet our definitions, standards, or expectations, we trash Him and look for another god that we can manipulate to suit our purposes and meet our needs. This is a serious control problem. When we attempt to maintain control, then we are going to have a problem. Giving up control is a central theme in the 12-step process:

Step One – We admit we are powerless over the "effect of our separation from God" that our lives had become unmanageable (original twelve steps say 'effect over alcohol').

Step Two – Come to believe that a power greater than ourselves could restore us to sanity.

Step Three – Make a decision to turn our will and our lives over to the care of God as we understand Him. And so forth...

The 12-step recovery model, when understood and applied correctly, has made, and continues to make a tremendous difference in the recovery process of thousands of people struggling to overcome addictions. Of course, it is important to remember and adhere to the familiar phrase: "It works, when you work it." I found the 12-step process helpful in my own spiritual growth.

Patient Question: I can't seem to move forward in my relationship with God because of my serious anger with Him. What can I do?

My Response: You are not alone in your anger with God. I then tell them my wife's story following our daughter's death. Kathy was very angry with God and had some hard questions for Him. Let me put it this way, she was not shy in expressing her anger over everything. She was angry and people around her knew it. A pastor friend of ours told me, "You know, He is a pretty big God. He has heard it before. He can handle it." I appreciated his input for it reminded me that anger is simply that... anger. It is a common emotional reaction to hurt. And my wife was very hurt. Problems arise when we repress

What Does It Mean?

our anger. It can morph into resentment and bitterness, which can plunge us into the black hole of depression that, of course, has potentially devastating effects on our internal world and how we relate to others.

Well, to make a long story short, Kathy, while pregnant, addressed her anger by spending hours, days, and months searching out the truth of God's Word, often while sitting at Melissa's gravesite. She had some long, very direct conversations with God. She asked Him, "Why do people die for you? What makes you so special?" She had been listening to many, many people share their sympathetic sentiments: "I'm sorry for your loss, but at least your daughter is now in heaven, or in a better place, or with your grandma." She had such a desire to know the truth of where Melissa was and who God was that her anger brought her to a place of passion, a passion for truth. After this extended time of intense searching and prayer, she came to a place of peace deep down in her heart. She concluded that people die for Him because He is the giver of life (John 5:24). She asked God for a renewed ability to love again. He showed Himself faithful. Kathy has not only a renewed ability to love, but she demonstrates authentic love for God and love for others, which is a witness of God's faithful love and grace!

Everyone will handle anger differently because everyone heals differently. But the fact still remains, if one wants to really move toward a relationship with God, they must face their anger, resentment, and bitterness. At times it might mean asking for help, but it is important to do whatever it takes to provide an opportunity to move toward spiritual health.

Patient Question: Did you notice that many of the people who influenced your spiritual direction were random people that didn't even really know you? Is that true for everyone?

My Response: No, it's not true for everyone. Since God has created each of us uniquely it makes sense that our journeys, though in many ways similar, will be different. Just like how my wife and I grieved the loss of our daughter differently, our spiritual journeys will look a bit different as well.

I must first point out that throughout my life I've had numerous people speak into my life and impact my spiritual formation. Family, friends, teachers, coaches, pastors, counselors, speakers, authors, and mentors have all spoken truth into my life, but each in a different way and with different effects.

What Does It Mean?

It is my observation that when we really take time to reflect upon some very significant turning points in our lives that have had a powerful impact on our spiritual formation, quite often seemingly "random" people and "random" circumstances are life-changing. Although the Scriptures tell us that God doesn't do things "randomly." He has a plan and purpose for all things (Psalm 37:23, Psalm 139:7-10, Psalm 23:2-4, Rom. 8:28).

It is not only encouraging, but challenging, to accept the idea that God does not waste anything. My actions, no matter how significant or insignificant they are, may have a direct bearing on another person's life, especially their spiritual journey.

God has a way of working things out and drawing us to Himself.

Discussion Question: What is the difference between solitude and isolation? How does each relate or affect one's spirituality?

My Response: I define isolation as "running away" and solitude as "running toward." Both isolation and solitude involve being alone. But isolation is not healthy and solitude is healthy. Isolation moves us away from our most valuable support, our friends, coworkers, family, and God, making us vulnerable to a "spiritual derailing," whereas solitude moves us toward our most valued support, God, which strengthens our spiritual life.

It is interesting that when a crisis, or a perceived crisis, occurs we have a tendency to want to isolate ourselves and hope it all goes away when the more beneficial response is to spend some time alone with God, in solitude, give Him our burden and listen to His still small voice. Solitude, then, becomes a step toward learning to trust, which generates faith, which in turn greatly enhances our spiritual life.

HOW IMPORTANT IS THIS STUFF?

THE PEACOCK FEATHER

At the conclusion of my lecture at the recovery center, I do a demonstration with a peacock feather. Now granted, I really don't know anything about peacocks, and I don't want to insinuate that they have some deep spiritual significance. It is simply a little illustration I use to conclude my presentation. Many people have told me that even after many years they remember the "peacock feather illustration."

I place the tip of the feather on the tip of my finger and stare down at the point where the feather is balancing on my finger. The feather begins to slowly sway back and forth. I point out that our life journey looks a bit like my balancing act as I walk around the room carefully staring at my finger while attempting to maintain the feather's balance as it sways.

I then stop and reset the feather on my finger and instead of looking down at my finger, I slowly look up at the beautiful eye of the feather, located at its very top. The feather no long sways back and forth, but instead stays very still (try it; you'll see what I mean).

As I stare at the eye, I explain how this balancing illustration reminds me of our spiritual journey. When we focus our attention on ourselves as we "do life," we are less secure. Sure, we create a balancing act, but it does not, in any way, represent peace, tranquility, or serenity. But when we keep our eyes (mind and heart) on our God we can experience a sense of balance, peace, and serenity that was impossible before.

An interesting observation is that while I am staring at the eye of the feather as it balances on my finger, and I then ask someone to take the feather away, the position of my eyes and hands still represent a posture of dependence, gratitude, and praise to God: my head and eyes are looking upward and my palms are facing up. Our relationship with God is the most important area of focus in all of life (Colossians 3:1-4, Hebrews 12:1-2a).

Final Thoughts

My life experience has been, and will continue to be, a series of ups and downs, pain and pleasure, sadness and joys, failures and achievements. My journey includes an authentic encounter with God, who has been seeking after me my entire life (Luke 19:10). The formation and direction of my life involves a relationship with Him and with other people. It is a process of learning to love and learning to trust and to obey. God has not wasted anything in my life, and I am GRATEFUL!

Below, I have provided some additional questions for you to think about. Wrestle with them. Pray over them. Meditate upon them. Share your journey with others.

I believe it is crucial that you address your own spiritual formation and recovery. And as you do this, may you discover, like I did, that even though I am a broken, sinful person with a recovering heart....

- I am loved and forgiven.
- I am significant.
- I matter A LOT to God.
- And He matters A LOT to me.

Inside YOUR Recovering Heart

ADDITIONAL QUESTIONS TO GUIDE YOU ALONG THE PATH

- How would you describe your spiritual formation and recovery? Outline your story, write your story, and then tell your story to someone else.
- How did your childhood influence your spiritual direction? Did you move toward God or away from God?
- Who or what influenced your understanding of spiritual things? Who influenced your spiritual direction?
- Have you ever had "random" people in your life who have influenced your spiritual direction? Who? When? How?
- Can you see how God was working throughout your adolescent years? How did you respond to God during those years?

- Have you ever had someone die who was very close to you? How was your spirituality impacted in your grieving and recovery process?
- Have you ever "walked away" from God? How did you come back to Him? Or are you still walking away? What needs to happen for God to get your attention?
- Are you struggling with "secret habits" that are hindering your walk with God?
- Have you ever struggled with pride or lust? Have you ever dealt with these things or are you still struggling? What did you do to overcome these (counseling, support groups, 12-steps)? Are there other problem areas in your life that you want to deal with? What are you doing to address them?
- Have you ever allowed people to speak into your life through mentoring or small groups?
- Have you ever spent time alone with God, reflecting on His love and grace and listening to His "still small voice"? How did God speak to your soul?
- Have you ever worked through the 12-step process? Are you familiar with the Serenity Prayer? The Lord's Prayer? How do these prayers speak to you?
- 1 John 1:9 states, "If we confess our sins, He is faithful and just and will forgive us our sins and purify us from all unrighteousness." Do you believe this?

Have you ever told God about your sins and asked Him to forgive you?

Wherever you are in your life journey, you might discover that you hear a knocking at the door of your heart. This happens by God's design.

Jesus said, "Here I am! I stand at the door and knock. If anyone hears my voice and opens the door, I will come in and eat with that person, and they with me" (Revelation 3:20).

God wants a relationship with us. He pursues us, but does not force Himself upon us. He stands at the door of our recovering heart and knocks.
Are you going to open the door and invite Him inside?

Appendix A

FURTHER STEPS FOR A RECOVERING HEART

Find a Mentor

Find someone who is farther along the path of recovery and who will guide you, nurture you, and teach you. This person will help you find and participate in a small group that meets your needs (i.e. church small group, Bible study group, Celebrate Recovery groups, GriefShare groups, The Genesis Process for Change groups, Pure Desire Groups, AA/NA/SA/ Al-Anon groups, et cetera). Remember: We can't do it alone!

Affirmations – Fill your Mind with God's Promises

Here are a few promises to get you started – 2 Peter 1:4, Jer.29:11, Matt 11:28-29, Is.40:29-31, Phil. 4:19, 7-39, Rom.8:37-39, Prov. 1:33, John 14:27, Heb. 13:5, Rom 10:9, Rom 6:23… and many more

Focused Prayer (A.C.T.S.)

Adoration-(Psalm 68:35)-Tell God how much you praise Him. Reflect upon His power and glory that is often seen in His creation: the sea, the mountains, the sunset. Praise the Lord!

Confession-(1 John 1:9)-Confession is simply agreeing with that which God already knows. There are no secrets with God. Tell Him how you have fallen short. Tell Him your secrets. And remember that He promises to cleanse us.

Thanksgiving-(1 Thessalonians 5:18)-There are many reasons to thank God. Don't forget to thank Him for His little gifts (i.e. birds singing, a playful pet, a smile from a baby, a butterfly, cool wind, warm sun, a blossom on a cherry tree, or a flower).

Supplication-(Philippians 4:6)-Tell God your wants and needs. He wants us to give Him our petitions. There is nothing too big or small to ask your loving Father. He cares about the details of our lives.

*Remember God always answers prayers according to His good purpose (yes, no, wait). Trust Him.

Appendix B

INFLUENCES AND RESOURCES FOR A RECOVERING HEART

God (Father, Son, and Holy Spirit)

I have no doubt that the number one influence in my spiritual formation and recovery is my relationship with God. God pursued me, I responded, He continues pursuing me, I continue to respond. He never gives up on me.

The Holy Bible

The Bible has consistently been my "go-to" as I have journeyed through life. The first book in the Bible I was drawn to was Proverbs. Some of the counselors at the basketball camp I attended in high school really spoke highly about the wisdom and life-changing words in this book. They were right.

The first Bible passage that I was drawn to on my own was Psalm 25. I was well into my double life season, and I continually turned to Psalm 25 as an attempt to get back on track.

If you have never read the Bible, I recommend starting in the first four books of the New Testament – the Gospel according to Matthew, Mark, Luke, and John or the book of Psalms. I suggest that you read the entire Bible at some point in your life.

Books for a Recovering Heart

Foster, Richard J. Celebration of Discipline: The Path to Spiritual Growth. Rev. 1st ed. San Francisco: Harper & Row, 1988.
Finding God – Larry Crabb, Zondervan Publishing, 1993
Freedom of Simplicity – Richard J. Foster, HarperCollins Publishers Inc., 1978
Knowing God – J.I.Packer, InterVarsity Press, 1973
Mere Christianity – C.S. Lewis, HarperCollins Publishers Inc., 1952
Recovering from the Losses of Life – H. Norman Wright, Fleming H. Revell (a division of Baker Publishing House), 2006

The Gift of Being Yourself – David G. Benner, InterVarsity Press, 2004,

The Knowledge of the Holy – A.W. Tozier, Harper and Row Publishers, 1961

The Life Recovery Bible – New Living Translation, Tynsdale House Publishers Inc., c. 2007

The Twelve Steps for Christians – Friends in Recovery, RPI Publishing Inc., 1994

The Renovation of the Heart – Dallas Willard, NavPress, 2002

Turn My Mourning into Dancing – Henri Nouwen, Thomas Nelson, 2001

For More Information About:
Kelly Baughman
Ministries and Availability
Contact Information and Blog
Visit: www.chaplainkelly.com

CPSIA information can be obtained
at www.ICGtesting.com
Printed in the USA
FSOW01n0242220715
9087FS